BASIC/NOT BORING
SCIENCE SKILLS

SCIENCE CONCEPTS & PROCESSES

Grades 4-5

Inventive Exercises to Sharpen
Skills and Raise Achievement

Series Concept & Development
by Imogene Forte & Marjorie Frank

Exercises by Marjorie Frank

Illustrations by Kathleen Bullock

Incentive Publications, Inc.
Nashville, Tennessee

About the cover:
Bound resist, or tie dye, is the most ancient known
method of fabric surface design. The brilliance of the
basic tie dye design on this cover reflects the possibilities
that emerge from the mastery of basic skills.

Cover art by Mary Patricia Deprez, dba Tye Dye Mary®
Cover design by Marta Drayton and Joe Shibley
Edited by Charlotte Bosarge

ISBN 0-86530-586-2

PRINTED IN THE UNITED STATES OF AMERICA
www.incentivepublications.com

TABLE OF CONTENTS

INTRODUCTION . . . Celebrate Basic Science Skills 7

    Skills Checklist for Science Investigations 8

SKILLS EXERCISES 10

    Science Everywhere You Look . . . (Nature of Science: Personal-Social Perspectives) .. 10

    Who Has It Right? . . . (Nature of Science) 12

    Which Branch Is Which? . . . (Branches of Science) 13

    Sorting Out Specialties . . . (Fields of Science) 14

    Great Inventions & Grand Discoveries . . . (Scientific Inventions & Discoveries) 16

    What Good Are They? . . . . . . (Scientific Inventions & Discoveries) 18

    Mysteries of History . . . (Science History) 20

    Talking Technology . . . (Science, Technology & Society) 22

    Serious Snooping . . . (Scientific Inquiry) 24

    Big Ideas . . . (Science Concepts) 26

    On the Lookout for Systems . . . (Science Concepts: Systems) 28

    An Orderly Business . . . (Science Concepts: Order & Organization) 29

    To Change or Not to Change? . . . (Science Concepts: Change & Constancy) 30

    What Led to What? . . . (Science Concepts: Cause & Effect) 32

    Good News About Whiskers . . . (Science Concepts: Form & Function) 34

A Friendship That Matters . . . (Science Concepts: Energy & Matter) 36

Nature Repeats Itself . . . (Science Concepts: Cycles) 38

Attention, Please! . . . (Science Processes: Observe) 40

Science is a Classy Subject . . . (Science Processes: Classify) 42

Smart Guessing . . . (Science Processes: Hypothesize) 44

Don't Forget the Math! . . . (Science Processes: Measure; Use Numbers) 46

Instead of the Real Thing . . . (Science Processes: Use Models) 47

What? Why? What Else? . . . (Science Processes: Infer & Predict;
                                       Interpret & Communicate) 48

Looking for Answers . . . (Science Processes: Design an Experiment) 50

Confusion in the Lab . . . (Science Processes: Investigate Safely) 52

APPENDIX 53

Terms for Science Concepts & Processes 54

Topics Studied by Some Fields of Science 55

Science Concepts & Processes Skills Test 56

Skills Test Answer Key 60

Answers to Exercises 61

CELEBRATE BASIC SCIENCE SKILLS

Basic does not mean boring! There is certainly nothing dull about . . .
  . . . searching for science in a backpack, on a skateboard, or in the shower.
  . . . snooping around to solve mysteries about pyramids, submarines, and safety pins.
  . . . showing off that you know the difference between an ichthyologist and a paleontologist.
  . . . exploring the wonders and talents of inventions like fax machines, neon, x-rays, and zippers.
  . . . investigating the behavior of spinning eggs, cats, and musical silverware.
  . . . experimenting with singing bottles, green bananas, and home-made carbon dioxide.
  . . . figuring out what's related to a boa constrictor or a hyena.

These are just some of the adventures students can explore as they celebrate basic science skills. The idea of celebrating the basics is just what it sounds like—enjoying and getting good at knowing the big ideas of science and the processes scientists use to understand the natural world. Each page invites learners to try a high-interest, appealing exercise that will sharpen or review one specific science skill, concept, or process. This is no ordinary fill-in-the-blanks way to learn material. These investigations are fun and surprising. Students will do the useful work of deepening science knowledge while they follow five clever scientists who lead them to explore science concepts and processes.

The pages in this book can be used in many ways:
- to sharpen or review a skill or concept with one student
- to reinforce the concept with a small or large group
- by students working independently
- by students working independently under the direction of a parent or teacher

Each page may be used to introduce a new concept or process to explore, to reinforce that idea, or to assess a student's understanding and performance. Beyond the twenty-six exercises, you will find an appendix of resources helpful to the student and teacher—including a glossary of terms used in the book and a ready-to-use test for assessing science concepts and processes.

The pages are written with the assumption that an adult will be available to assist the student with his or her learning. It will be helpful for students to have access to science resources, textbooks, encyclopedias, library books, and Internet reference sources.

As your students take on the challenges of these adventures with science concepts and processes, they will grow. As you watch them check off the basic science skills they have sharpened and standards they have mastered, you can celebrate with them!

The Skills Test (pages 56–59)
Use the skills test as a pre-test or post-test. This will help you check the students' mastery of the basic skills and understandings in the area of science concepts and processes. It can also help prepare them for further success on tests of standards, instructional goals, or other individual achievement.

SKILLS CHECKLIST FOR
SCIENCE CONCEPTS, Grades 4-5

✔	SKILL	PAGE(S)
	Show understanding of the presence of science in everyday life; Identify ways science impacts personal life; Identify some uses of technology	10–11
	Show understanding of the nature of science research, ideas, and discoveries	10–12, 18–19
	Show understanding of science as a human endeavor	10, 12
	Show understanding of the limitations of science	12
	Distinguish among the branches of science; Identify the topics and fields associated with different branches of science	13
	Distinguish among the fields of science	14–15
	Identify some key scientific inventions and discoveries	16–17
	Recognize the use and significance of some scientific inventions and discoveries	18–19
	Identify some key events and sequences in the history of science	20–21
	Show understanding of the impact of science and technology on Earth and human life; Recognize that scientific-technological inventions and changes have costs and benefits	22–23
	Show understanding of the nature and method of scientific inquiry	24–25
	Recognize and distinguish among some key science concepts	26–27
	Show understanding of the science concept of systems	28
	Show understanding of the science concepts of order and organization	29
	Show understanding of the science concepts of change and constancy	30–31
	Show understanding of the science concept of cause and effect	32–33
	Show understanding of the science concept of the relationship between form and function	34–35
	Show understanding of the science concept of the relationship between energy and matter	36–37
	Show understanding of the science concept of cycle	38–39
	Understand and use the science process of observation	40–41
	Understand and use the science process of classification	42–43
	Understand and use the science process of forming a hypothesis	44–45
	Understand and use the science process of measuring and using numbers	46
	Understand and use the science process of using models	47
	Understand and use the science process of making inferences and predictions from data	48–49
	Understand and use the science process of interpreting and communicating results	49–49
	Understand and use the science process of designing an experiment	50–51
	Recognize some safety procedures for science investigation and experimentation	52

SCIENCE
CONCEPTS

Skills Exercises

SCIENCE EVERYWHERE YOU LOOK

Look around! It's everywhere! Science can be found in all kinds of places. Search for science in the places and spaces in your life!

Describe one way that science can be found in each of these places.

1. in the shower
_____
_____
_____

4. at the winter Olympics
_____
_____
_____

2. at a movie theater
_____
_____
_____

5. at the summer Olympics
_____
_____
_____

3. in a fish tank
_____
_____
_____

6. on a skateboard
_____
_____
_____

Use with page 11.

Name

7. at a basketball game

_____

_____

_____

_____

11. at a bowling alley

_____

_____

_____

_____

8. at an airport

_____

_____

_____

_____

12. in your backpack

_____

_____

_____

_____

9. on the freeway

_____

_____

_____

_____

13. in a canoe

_____

_____

_____

_____

10. in your kitchen

_____

_____

_____

_____

14. on a city street

_____

_____

_____

_____

Use with page 10.

Name

WHO HAS IT RIGHT?

Lawrence Leapfrog and Lester Lilypad are always arguing about who's smarter in science. For each of the following statements, only one of them has it right. Read both statements with the same number (for example: 1 and 1, or 2 and 2). Circle the one that is correct.

1. Science is the study of the ways the universe works.

2. Many scientific ideas are true, but some might be proven wrong.

3. Different fields of science often overlap with each other.

4. Math is rarely needed for science investigations.

5. People in many different kinds of work have made important science discoveries.

6. Scientific discoveries began in the 19th century.

7. Most scientists work in teams.

8. When scientists work, they ignore their personal beliefs.

9. Scientists work in many different locations.

10. There are many problems that science cannot solve.

1. Science is the study of living things.

2. All scientific ideas are true.

3. Different fields of science are very separate from each other.

4. Math is needed for many science investigations.

5. All important scientific discoveries are made by scientists.

6. Scientific discoveries began thousands of years ago.

7. Most scientists work alone.

8. When scientists work, their personal beliefs affect their work.

9. Scientists work only in laboratories.

10. Science will eventually solve all human problems.

Lawrence

Lester

I'm right!

Prove it!

Name

WHICH BRANCH IS WHICH?

I have spent my whole life studying in the branch of **LIFE SCIENCE**. I investigate all of life! I know about plants, animals, cells, the human body, diseases and cures, birth, growth, and death. I know about how all life is related to other lives and to the whole planet.

My branch is **PHYSICAL SCIENCE**. These are the fields that study all about matter: atoms, molecules, elements and compounds—and the way they mix and react with one another! We also study energy, motion, forces and work, heat, light, sound, and electricity.

Well, without **EARTH & SPACE SCIENCE**, you two would have nothing to study! My branch includes fields that study the entire universe. We find out about the Earth and other objects in space!

L
(Life Science)

P
(Physical Science)

E–S
(Earth & Space Science)

Read about three of the main branches of science (above). There are many, many fields (areas) within each branch. A few of them are shown below.

Find out about each field listed here. Which fields belong to which branches? Write *P*, *E-S*, or *L* for the branch that matches each field.

___ 1. BIOLOGY

___ 2. AERONAUTICS

___ 3. MICROBIOLOGY

___ 4. OCEANOGRAPHY

___ 5. ANATOMY

___ 6. BOTANY

___ 7. SEISMOLOGY

___ 8. ECOLOGY

___ 9. ASTRONOMY

___ 10. GENETICS

___ 11. PHYSICS

___ 12. NUCLEAR PHYSICS

___ 13. GEOLOGY

___ 14. CHEMISTRY

___ 15. ZOOLOGY

Name

SORTING OUT SPECIALTIES

There are dozens of different kinds of scientists—all asking questions about the way the world works. Different scientists study different things. These are called fields of science. Here are a few scientific fields. Choose the best answer to show what each different scientist would study.

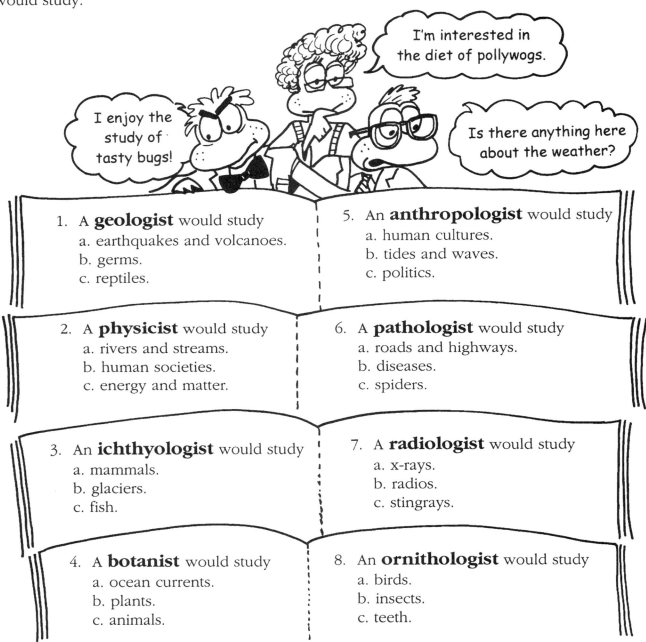

1. A **geologist** would study
   a. earthquakes and volcanoes.
   b. germs.
   c. reptiles.

2. A **physicist** would study
   a. rivers and streams.
   b. human societies.
   c. energy and matter.

3. An **ichthyologist** would study
   a. mammals.
   b. glaciers.
   c. fish.

4. A **botanist** would study
   a. ocean currents.
   b. plants.
   c. animals.

5. An **anthropologist** would study
   a. human cultures.
   b. tides and waves.
   c. politics.

6. A **pathologist** would study
   a. roads and highways.
   b. diseases.
   c. spiders.

7. A **radiologist** would study
   a. x-rays.
   b. radios.
   c. stingrays.

8. An **ornithologist** would study
   a. birds.
   b. insects.
   c. teeth.

Use with page 15.

Name

9. A **geneticist** would study
   a. fossils.
   b. electric generators.
   c. human DNA.

10. An **ecologist** would study
   a. financial systems.
   b. pollution.
   c. brain surgery.

11. A **cytologist** would study
   a. cycles.
   b. cells.
   c. clouds.

12. A **seismologist** would study
   a. earthquakes.
   b. nuclear reactions.
   c. brain waves.

13. A **zoologist** would study
   a. old ruins.
   b. volcanoes.
   c. animals.

14. A **meteorologist** would study
   a. meteors.
   b. tumors.
   c. weather.

15. A **chemist** would study
   a. elements and compounds.
   b. butterfly life cycles.
   c. amphibians.

16. An **astronomer** would study
   a. fortune-telling.
   b. comets and supernovas.
   c. prehistoric animals.

17. An **hematologist** would study
   a. hermits.
   b. snakes.
   c. blood.

18. A **paleontologist** would study
   a. behavior of water.
   b. fossils.
   c. bacteria.

19. A **psychologist** would study
   a. floods and tornados.
   b. human behavior.
   c. dinosaurs.

20. An **entomologist** would study
   a. the development of language.
   b. word endings.
   c. beetles and flies.

21. A **physiologist** would study
   a. fizzy liquids.
   b. body processes.
   c. seedless plants.

Use with page 14.

Name

15 *Basic Skills/Science Concepts & Processes 4-5*

GREAT INVENTIONS & GRAND DISCOVERIES

Thousands of inventions and discoveries fill the science books. Here are just a few of the most dazzling and memorable! Look at the names of these discoveries and inventions. Which one is described in each example? Write the name next to the description.

1. In the 1500s, Gerardus Mercator found a way to show the Earth's surface on pieces of paper.

   _____

2. Robert Hook invented a special tube for viewing tiny objects in the 1600s.

   _____

3. About 6000 years ago, ancient cultures figured out that a round device could make it easier to haul heavy things. This changed transportation forever.

   _____

4. In 1602, an invention by Galileo Galilei allowed him to see the surface of the moon.

   _____

5. Johannes Gutenberg invented a machine in the mid-1400s. After that, books could be made more quickly.

   _____

6. A 1920 discovery by Dr. Alexander Fleming helps people recover from serious infections.

   _____

7. In 1783, a Frenchman named Louis Lenormand invented a device that made it possible for people to float through the air.

   _____

8. Ferdinand Carre's 1858 invention changed the way food was stored.

   _____

SUBMARINE

paper   electricity

sewing machine

printing press

MAPS

PARACHUTE

steam engine   refrigerator

FLURP   GLUB

space capsule

X-RAYS

frozen food process

penicillin

Use with page 17.

Name _____

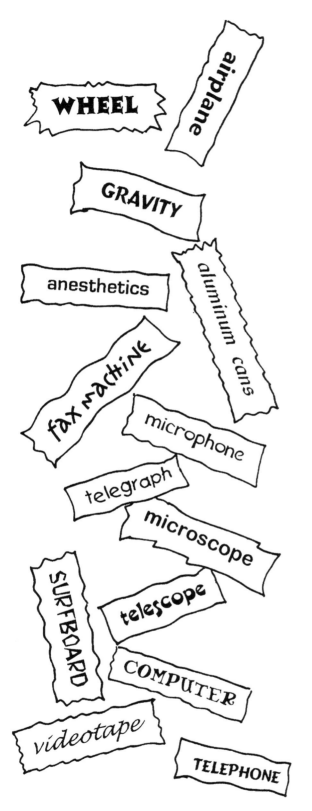

9. This 1925 invention of Clarence Birdseye again changed the way food could be stored.

   _____

10. In 1904, a German scientist named Arthur Korn invented a way to send writing and pictures across a telephone line.

   _____

11. Benjamin Franklin was flying a kite in a thunderstorm in 1752 when he made this discovery.

   _____

12. An American dentist, William Morton, found a way to put patients to sleep during surgery. This 1846 discovery helped patients avoid a lot of pain!

   _____

13. This 1838 invention of Elias Howe really sped up the production of clothing and other things made from fabric.

   _____

14. In 1838 Samuel Morse invented a handy way to use bursts of electricity to send messages long distances over a wire.

   _____

15. Isaac Newton made this discovery in 1687 when an apple fell on his head.

   _____

16. An 1898 invention by John P. Holland gave people a brand new way to travel through water.

   _____

17. Before the Chinese invented this idea 2000 years ago, people had to write on animal skins or carve words into wood or stone.

   _____

18. Doctors have been able to see many things inside bodies since this accidental discovery in 1905 by German Scientist Wilhelm Konrad von Roentgen.

   _____

Use with page 16.

Name _____

WHAT GOOD ARE THEY?

It's fine to know about great discoveries and inventions. It's even better to know how they are useful or helpful, or how they have changed things in the world.

DISCOVERIES

1. the discovery of **antibodies**

   _____
   _____
   _____

2. the discovery of **fire**

   _____
   _____
   _____

3. the discovery of **gravity**

   _____
   _____
   _____

4. the discovery of **the planet Mars**

   _____
   _____
   _____

5. the discovery of **neon**

   _____
   _____
   _____

Think about each of these discoveries and inventions. Write a short description of how each one has been helpful or useful.

6. **YOU name a discovery.**

   Discovery _____

   What good is it?

   _____
   _____
   _____

Use with page 19.

Name

INVENTIONS

7. the invention of the **helicopter**

_____

_____

_____

8. the invention of the **zipper**

_____

_____

_____

9. the invention of **plastic**

_____

_____

_____

10. the invention of **vaccines**

_____

_____

_____

11. the invention of **margarine**

_____

_____

_____

12. the invention of **barbed wire**

_____

_____

_____

13. the invention of **CDs (compact discs)**

_____

_____

_____

14. **YOU name an invention.**

Invention _____

What good is it?

_____

_____

_____

The combustion engine is one of my favorite inventions!

Putt Putt

Use with page 18.

Name _____

19   _Basic Skills/Science Concepts & Processes 4-5_

MYSTERIES OF HISTORY

Freida and other students of science spend lot of time tracking down mysterious events and unanswered questions. Do your own snooping to find out about some past events in science.

Sometimes a scientist is a super detective. Solve these mysteries of science history. Choose one or more correct answers.

Mystery #1

Which was developed before automobiles?

a. helicopters

b. trains

c. airplanes

d. cameras

Mystery #3

Which came first?

a. telephones

b. electric light bulbs

c. submarines

d. the pyramids

Mystery #2

Which invention is most recent?

a. ice cream

b. cell phone

c. computer

d. sewing machine

Mystery #4

Copernicus believed that

a. air is heavier than water.

b. the Earth is round.

c. diseases are caused by germs.

Mystery #5

Isaac Newton made discoveries about

a. motion and force.

b. earthquakes.

c. microbiology

d. earthworms.

Use with page 21.

Name

Mystery #6

Which discovery came first?

a. fire

b. gravity

c. the planet Jupiter

d. the atom

Mystery #7

What invention from the 1940s and 1950s allowed food to cook faster?

a. fire

b. microwave oven

c. counter-top stove

d. charcoal stove

Mystery #8

Which was NOT invented before 1900?

a. camera

b. bicycle

c. helicopter

d. safety pin

e. calendar

Mystery #9

Who invented a camera that would take moving pictures?

a. Walt Disney

b. Louis Pasteur

c. Alexander G. Bell

d. Thomas Edison

Mystery #10

Who discovered the element that led to producing atomic energy?

a. Marie Curie

b. Pierre Curie

c. Benjamin Franklin

d. Eli Whitney

Mystery #11

Which was invented since rockets?

a. DVD players

b. paper

c. ATMs

d. VCRs

Mystery #12

What 1902 invention by Willis Carrier changed the way we live and work?

a. vacuum cleaner

b. locks

c. air conditioner

d. radio

Use with page 20.

Name

TALKING TECHNOLOGY

Every day around the world, science is put to use with tools and tricks that surprise us and change our lives. Two things come along with each new tool or process of technology: benefits and costs.

Costs include more than just money. There are many kinds of costs that may include job losses, health risks, damage to the environment, harm to people, or other negative consequences. Write one benefit and one cost for each of these tools of technology:

1. ATM (Automatic Teller Machine)

Benefit _____

Cost_____

2. camera

Benefit_____

Cost _____

3. credit card

Benefit_____

Cost _____

4. jet engines

Benefit _____

Cost _____

5. email

Benefit_____

Cost _____

Technology is anything that puts science to work. It can be a machine, tool, gadget, or process—anything that applies science to a practical use in the real world!

Use with page 23.

Name _____

6. gunpowder

Benefit_____

Cost _____

7. airports close to cities

Benefit _____

Cost_____

8. whipped cream that squirts out of a can

Benefit_____

Cost _____

9. rocket

Benefit_____

Cost _____

10. plastic milk containers

Benefit_____

Cost _____

11. videotape

Benefit_____

Cost _____

12. You name a device, machine, tool, invention, or process of technology. Then describe a benefit and a cost.

Device or process _____

Benefit_____

Cost _____

Use with page 22.

Name _____

SERIOUS SNOOPING

Questions are a big part of science. Like other scientists and science students, Frederick follows some clear steps when he looks for answers. This process (group of steps) is called the scientific method, or scientific inquiry.

THE GREAT BANANA STAKE-OUT

Frederick bought a lot of bananas. Sometimes he left them in the fruit basket on the counter. Sometimes he kept them in a paper or plastic bag. He noticed that the bananas he kept in bags seemed to ripen more slowly than the ones he left out. The bananas in the fruit basket seemed to ripen very fast. He wondered what might cause some bananas to ripen faster than others. He guessed that bananas would ripen fastest if they were exposed to air or if they were touching other bananas.

He decided to plan a careful investigation. He bought 15 green bananas, paper bags, plastic bags, tape, and a few ripe bananas. Frederick planned 8 different ways to store the bananas. He put 1 green banana in a paper bag and 1 green banana in a plastic bag. Then he put 2 green bananas in a paper bag and 2 green bananas in a plastic bag. Next, he put 1 green banana in a paper bag with a ripe banana and 1 green banana in a plastic bag with a ripe banana. He sealed all the bags tightly with tape. Last, he laid 6 green bananas in the fruit basket on top of some ripe bananas and 1 green banana alone on the counter.

Then Frederick started a "stake-out" to watch the bananas carefully. He checked them every day and made a table to keep track of his results. He wrote down the number of days it took for each green banana or group of green bananas to get ripe (turn yellow with brown spots).

When all the bananas had ripened, he looked at his results. The bananas in the basket with ripe bananas ripened the fastest. The lone banana out in the air ripened fast also. The bananas in the paper bags ripened faster than bananas in plastic bags. Bananas that were stored with other bananas ripened faster than those that were alone. Bananas with ripe bananas ripened even faster than those with other green bananas.

Frederick drew a poster to show all the test groups, and wrote the number of days it took each to ripen. He thought the results showed that keeping bananas away from air slowed the ripening. He also concluded that when bananas ripen, they must give off some chemical that affects other bananas nearby.

When he finished, Frederick had more questions. He wondered if opening the paper bags to check the bananas let in air that affected the results. He wondered how fast green bananas would ripen in the fruit basket if there were no ripe bananas to touch. He also wondered how fast bananas would ripen if they were put in the refrigerator.

As soon as I finish this inquiry, I'm going to make a banana cream pie!

Use with page 25.

Name

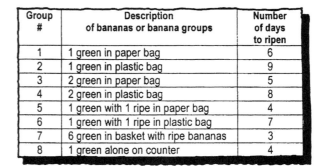

Read the description of the inquiry that I've been doing. Then answer the questions about the scientific inquiry process.

Group #	Description of bananas or banana groups	Number of days to ripen
1	1 green in paper bag	6
2	1 green in plastic bag	9
3	2 green in paper bag	5
4	2 green in plastic bag	8
5	1 green with 1 ripe in paper bag	4
6	1 green with 1 ripe in plastic bag	7
7	6 green in basket with ripe bananas	3
8	1 green alone on counter	4

STEP 1 – OBSERVE: *What observation led Frederick to do an experiment?*

_____

STEP 2 – ASK QUESTIONS: *What question did he want to answer?*

_____

STEP 3 – HYPOTHESIZE: *What "smart guess" did he make about what would happen?*

_____

STEP 4 – PLAN AND CARRY OUT AN EXPERIMENT: *What plan did he follow?*

_____

STEP 5 – GATHER DATA (INFORMATION): *What supplies did he use? How did he collect the data?*

_____

STEP 6 – INTERPRET DATA: *What results did he find?*

_____

STEP 7 – GIVE EXPLANATIONS: *What explanation did he give for the results?*

_____

STEP 8 – COMMUNICATE RESULTS: *How did he show or share the results?*

_____

STEP 9 – OFFER OTHER QUESTIONS: *What other questions did he have when the experiment was done?*

_____

Use with page 24.

Name

BIG IDEAS

Professor Gracie Gravity talks to students about all different kinds of science. She and her students keep running into some **big ideas** that stretch across many science topics. Read the list of big science ideas. The class is discussing several science events and personal stories. Match each of these to the big ideas shown on these two pages. Write the number (1–16) in front of one or more science concepts that relates to the example.

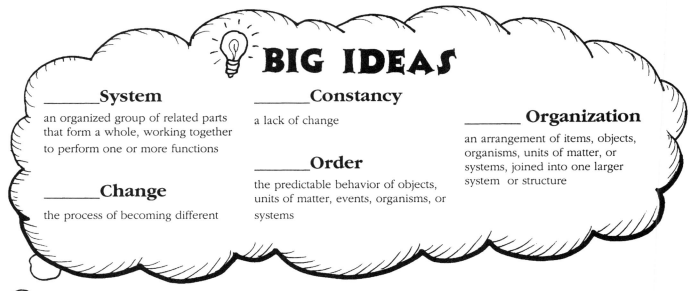

BIG IDEAS

_____ **System**
an organized group of related parts that form a whole, working together to perform one or more functions

_____ **Change**
the process of becoming different

_____ **Constancy**
a lack of change

_____ **Order**
the predictable behavior of objects, units of matter, events, organisms, or systems

_____ **Organization**
an arrangement of items, objects, organisms, units of matter, or systems, joined into one larger system or structure

Events being discussed:

1. Axel forgot to put his box of fudge bars in the freezer when he came home from the store. They all melted!

2. When she visits the ocean, Lucy enjoys following the tide tables so that she can watch the high tides and low tides every day.

3. After Max eats his favorite artichoke pizza, it takes many body organs working together to digest the food and turn it into the energy his body needs.

4. Giant stars swell up into huge supergiants and eventually blow up with a grand explosion called a supernova.

5. A hip joint is actually a ball and socket. The upper leg bone has a rounded end that fits into a hollow space in the hip bone. This allows the leg to rotate in a circle.

6. Roxie notices that her new water heater is wrapped with a thick blanket of insulation to keep the water heater from losing heat.

Use with page 27.

Name _____

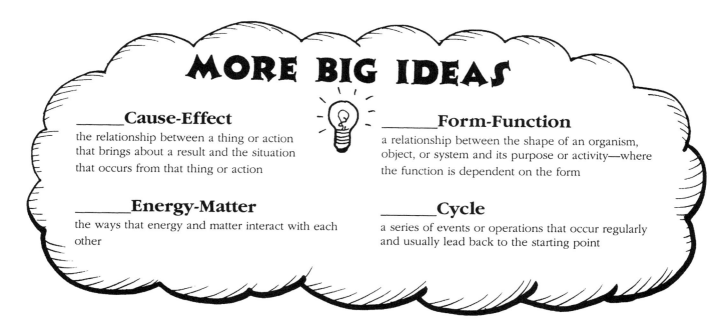

MORE BIG IDEAS

_____Cause-Effect
the relationship between a thing or action that brings about a result and the situation that occurs from that thing or action

_____Form-Function
a relationship between the shape of an organism, object, or system and its purpose or activity—where the function is dependent on the form

_____Energy-Matter
the ways that energy and matter interact with each other

_____Cycle
a series of events or operations that occur regularly and usually lead back to the starting point

7. Earth follows the same orbit around the sun, year after year.

8. A strong wind blew some pollen up Leonard's nose. Leonard sneezed.

9. As a soccer ball comes across the field toward Francine, her eyes see the ball and send a message to her brain. Her brain sends a message to her foot to kick the ball.

10. A bobsled is made in a very slim, sleek shape. It looks a lot like a bullet. This shape allows the sled to travel very fast.

11. In some places on the earth, mud, and clay are under great heat and pressure for years. Eventually they turn into a rock called slate.

12. In front of Tad's oceanfront home, the crashing waves pick up sand from the beach and move it along the shore, depositing it somewhere else.

13. Every year the Canadian geese fly south for the winter and return to their northern homes when the weather gets warm.

14. There are five classes of vertebrates. Each class shares certain characteristics. Example: all animals in the reptile class have scales, are cold-blooded, and breathe with lungs.

15. Animals and people give off carbon dioxide when they breathe. Plants take in the carbon dioxide and use it to make oxygen, which they give off. This is convenient, because animals and people need to take oxygen into their bodies to live.

16. Zeke has been very curious about snowflakes, so he captures them on a cold surface and examines them under the microscope. He is amazed to find that every snowflake has six points.

Use with page 26.

Name

ON THE LOOKOUT FOR SYSTEMS

A **SYSTEM**
is an organized group of
related parts that form
a whole, working together to
perform one or more functions.

The world is full of systems. Some of these exist naturally. Humans make some of them. Some are very simple—like a one-celled animal. Some are very complex—like the whole ecosystem of a desert.

Every system has parts and boundaries. (The boundaries are ways the system is separate from other systems.) Every system has something that goes into it (input) and something that comes out (output).

Fill in the missing information about systems 1, 2, and 3.

Example:

The system: *a muscle cell*

Some of its parts: *cell membrane, nucleus, cytoplasm*

Input: *nutrients, oxygen*

Output: *energy to the body, wastes (CO_2)*

1.

The system: *the respiratory system*

Some of its parts:

Input:

Output: *energy, carbon dioxide*

2.

The system: *a green plant*

Some of its parts:

Input:

Output:

3.

The system: *an electric circuit*

Some of its parts:

Input:

Output:

Name

AN ORDERLY BUSINESS

Answer the questions or follow the instructions for each example about order or organization.

ORDER
is the predictable behavior of objects, units of matter, events, organisms, or systems.

ORGANIZATION
is an arrangement of independent items, objects, organisms, units of matter, or systems—joined into one whole system or structure.

1. Molecules of water are cooled to a temperature below 32° F. What behavior can you expect from these molecules?

_____

_____

2. Fall is coming to a forest in the northern U.S.A. What are the squirrels likely to be doing?

_____

_____

3. These are organisms in a food chain. Number them in the order they would be found in the food chain. Begin with the producer as number 1.

_____ owl

_____ caterpillar

_____ mouse

_____ green leaf

_____ fox

_____ snake

4. The animal kingdom is organized into two major divisions. What are they?

_____

_____

5. Seed-bearing plants are organized into two major divisions. What are they?

_____

_____

6. What is the organization of the solar system? Number the planets in the order they are found in relation to the sun. Write number 1 next to the planet that is closest to the sun.

_____ Neptune		_____ Pluto
_____ Jupiter		_____ Venus
_____ Mars		_____ Mercury
_____ Earth		_____ Uranus
		_____ Saturn

Name

TO CHANGE OR NOT TO CHANGE?

CHANGE
is the process of
becoming different.

CONSTANCY
is a lack of change.

Archie sees change going all around him all the time. Sometimes there is so much change that it makes his head spin! Things change in size, shape, weight, purpose, position, and form.

But in the middle of a lot of change, some things stay constant. They keep doing the same thing, or their properties remain the same.

Read the examples on page 31 (A-J). Find examples that fit each description below.

Write the letter of the example on the line. Any letter (A-J) might fit in more than one place.

_____ 1. **change in physical properties** *(change in size, shape, or weight)*

_____ 2. **change in chemical make-up** *(substance becomes a new substance)*

_____ 3. **change in state or form** *(change in state of matter)*

_____ 4. **change in position** *(moves from one place to another)*

_____ 5. **transfer of energy** *(energy moves from one source to another)*

_____ 6. **constancy** *(a lack of change)*

Use with page 31.

Name

A. Archie's little sister sits still on a swing. He runs up behind her and pushes the swing high above his head as he runs under it. He stops running. The swing continues to go back and forth for a long time.

B. Archie puts ice cream, chocolate syrup, and milk in a blender and mixes up a wonderful, thick milkshake.

C. Archie didn't intend to swallow that gumball whole. He popped it into his mouth. The next thing he knew, it had slithered down his esophagus into his stomach!

D. First Archie mixes flour, sugar, eggs, milk, lemon juice, and baking powder for several minutes with an electric mixer. Then he pours the mixture in a pan and bakes it in the oven. He's quite happy to eat the cake that's done 30 minutes later.

E. Absent-minded Archie left his bicycle outside all winter. By May the bike was covered with rust.

F. Oops! Archie dropped the bag of groceries! The big jar of peanuts turned into a heap of broken glass and smashed peanuts.

G. It's predictable! In every 24-hour period, the Earth will make one complete rotation.

H. Archie rushes into the ski lodge, tears off his gloves, and holds his hands in front of the fireplace. In a few minutes, his cold fingers are warm as toast.

I. Archie puts a stick of butter in the microwave. In just 30 seconds, it was completely melted.

J. Archie watches as a strong wind pushes the beach sand into high dunes.

YOU Think About It!

7. Name something in the natural world or human-made world that **remains constant.**

_____

8. Describe something that shows a change in **physical properties.**

_____

9. Describe something that shows a change in **chemical make-up.**

_____

10. Describe something that shows a change in **position.**

_____

11. Describe something that shows a change in **state or form.**

_____

12. Describe something that shows a transfer of **energy.**

_____

uh, oh!

Use with page 30.

Name

WHAT LED TO WHAT?

CAUSE & EFFECT

A cause is anything that brings about a result. An effect is the result (the event or situation that follows from the cause).

It seems to Roxie that one event always happens because of another! She's right. In the natural world as well as the world of human-made things, events cause other events. Sometimes she has to stop and look hard to understand what causes led to what effects and what effects resulted from what causes!

Examine these examples. Look hard at each one to figure out what is the cause and what is the effect. Write at least one cause and effect pair for each example (1–5). There may be more than one possible pair for some of the examples.

1. Hot magma gushes out from inside a crack in the earth, forming a volcano.

cause _____

_____

effect _____

_____

2. Pumice stone is a volcanic rock that is very light weight with many air pockets. Hot, melted lava from a volcano cooled very quickly, trapping lots of air inside the rock.

cause _____

effect _____

3. Mortimer used to have a resting heart rate of 85 beats per minute. After running faithfully for 6 months, his resting heart rate has fallen to 70 beats per minute.

cause _____

effect _____

Use with page 33.

Name

4. A singer used her voice so much that bumps formed on her vocal cords and her voice became very hoarse and scratchy.

cause _____

_____

effect _____

_____

5. A rattlesnake senses the presence of a predator and rattles its tail. The predator hears the warning and runs away.

cause _____

_____

effect _____

_____

6–7: Write a possible effect for the cause.

6. **cause:** Water seeps into the cracks of a rock and freezes.

possible effect: _____

_____

7. **cause:** Someone gets a cracker crumb caught in her windpipe.

possible effect: _____

_____

8–9: Write a possible cause for the effect.

8. **possible cause:** _____

_____

effect: Axel's strep throat bacteria gets knocked out.

9. **possible cause:** _____

_____

effect: A meteoroid becomes a meteor.
(This means that the meteoroid begins to burn.)

10. **YOU** write a cause and effect pair:

cause _____

_____

effect _____

_____

Use with page 32.

Name

GOOD NEWS ABOUT WHISKERS

FORM & FUNCTION

The form (shape or properties) of an object, organism, or system is often related to its operation (function). In many cases, what something can do (its function) is a direct result of its shape or properties (its form).

Read these form-function pairs. Think about how the function is dependent upon the form. Write the missing descriptions of the form or function for each one.

A cat has whiskers that are long and thin, and they're attached to nerves in the skin. This makes them sensitive to the touch, so a cat can "feel" places and spaces with its whiskers.

Catfish live on the bottom of lakes and other bodies of water. Their long feelers (whiskers) around their mouths help them to dig food from the muddy bottom.

Seals have long whiskers that are sensitive to touch. Their whiskers help them feel around and find food.

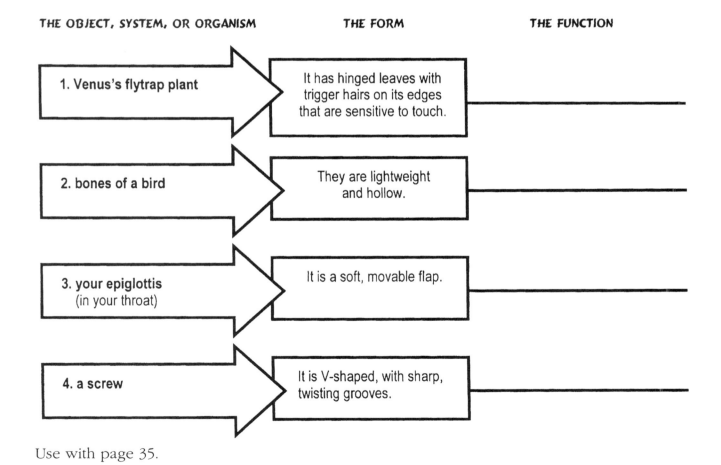

THE OBJECT, SYSTEM, OR ORGANISM	THE FORM	THE FUNCTION
1. Venus's flytrap plant	It has hinged leaves with trigger hairs on its edges that are sensitive to touch.	
2. bones of a bird	They are lightweight and hollow.	
3. your epiglottis (in your throat)	It is a soft, movable flap.	
4. a screw	It is V-shaped, with sharp, twisting grooves.	

Use with page 35.

Name

THE OBJECT, SYSTEM, OR ORGANISM	THE FORM	THE FUNCTION

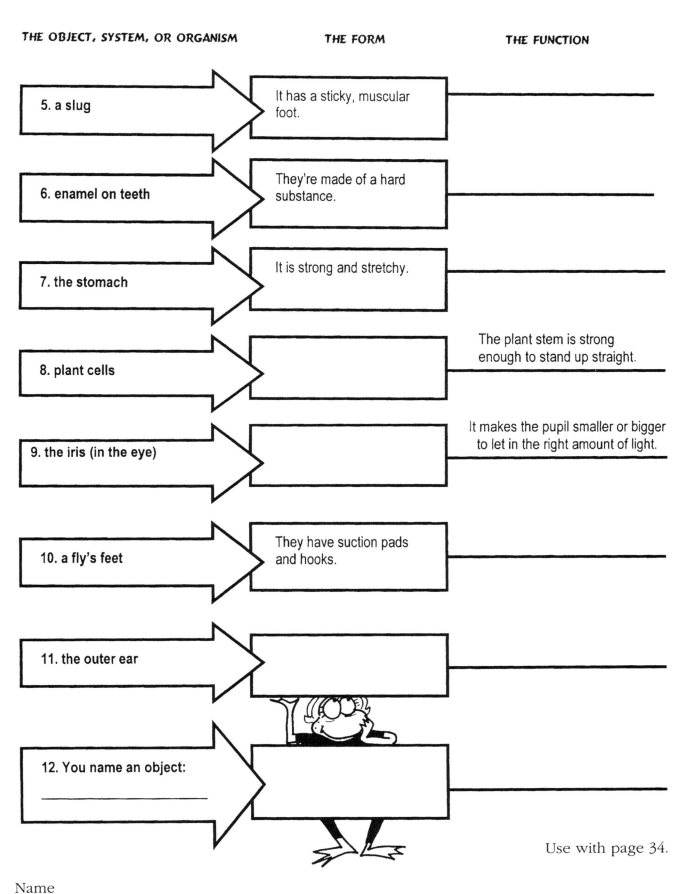

5. a slug — It has a sticky, muscular foot.

6. enamel on teeth — They're made of a hard substance.

7. the stomach — It is strong and stretchy.

8. plant cells — — The plant stem is strong enough to stand up straight.

9. the iris (in the eye) — — It makes the pupil smaller or bigger to let in the right amount of light.

10. a fly's feet — They have suction pads and hooks.

11. the outer ear —

12. You name an object: _____ —

Use with page 34.

Name

35   *Basic Skills/Science Concepts & Processes 4-5*

A FRIENDSHIP THAT MATTERS

Leonardo and Maxie have been observing interactions between energy and matter. They are having fun emailing their observations back and forth.

Read each tale. Identify the energy and the matter in each example. Then tell what will happen. (What will be the result of the interaction?)

ENERGY-MATTER

Energy and matter are closely related. They are constantly interacting with each other. This means that they affect one another or work together. Energy can move or change matter. Matter can be changed into energy. Energy can be transferred to matter.

1. I've been lying in the hot sunshine for 7 hours— without any sunscreen!

The **matter** is_____

The **energy** is_____

What will happen?_____

Example:

The baseball is pitched straight toward me. It connects with the bat and I hit it at full force!

The **matter** is _base ball_

The **energy** is _muscle power_

What will happen? _ball will sail_
through air

2. A huge, heavy branch has just broken off the tree in my front yard.

The **matter** is_____

The **energy** is_____

What will happen?_____

3. I've just thrown a handful of popcorn kernels into a hot campfire.

The **matter** is_____

The **energy** is_____

What will happen?_____

Use with page 37.

Name

4. The tug-of-war has started. My team has much less strength and weight than the other team.

The **matter** is_____

The **energy** is_____

What will happen?_____

5. Oh, no! I left my raft on the beach at the edge of the water. A huge wave is just approaching the raft.

The **matter** is_____

The **energy** is_____

What will happen?_____

6. A small cabin is right in the path of that tornado.

The **matter** is_____

The **energy** is_____

What will happen?_____

7. I watched as a satellite was launched into space. The satellite was taken to a place where it could orbit Earth, and the rocket is no longer carrying it.

The **matter** is_____

The **energy** is_____

What will happen?_____

8. I was drying my wet hat by holding it out the car window. Oops! I just let go of the hat!

The **matter** is_____

The **energy** is_____

What will happen?_____

9. You do one! Write your own example of an interaction between matter and energy.

The **matter** is_____

The **energy** is_____

Describe the **interaction**:_____

_____

_____

Use with page 36.

NATURE REPEATS ITSELF

Cycles are so common in the world that they often go without notice. Start noticing the cycles around you!

Write a short description of each of these cycles.

CYCLE

is a series of events or operations that occur regularly, and usually lead back to the starting point.

1. **Life Cycle of a Butterfly**

2. **Oxygen-Carbon Dioxide Cycle**

Use with page 39.

Name

3. Life Cycle of a Frog

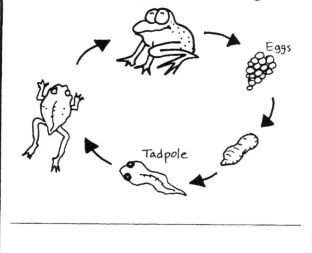

_____

_____

_____

_____

_____

4. Moon Phases

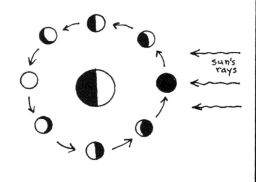

sun's rays

_____

_____

_____

_____

_____

_____

5. Earth's Revolution

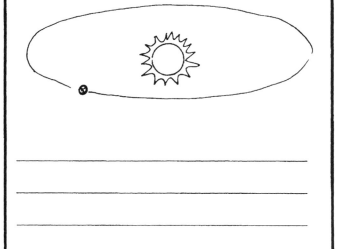

_____

_____

_____

_____

Name 3 other cycles you see in the world.

1._____

2._____

3._____

Use with page 38.

Name

ATTENTION, PLEASE!

What do you observe in each situation below? Write your observations on the little note pads next to each example.

Observe with all your senses: smell, taste, hearing, sight, and touch.

To OBSERVE
is to recognize and take note of facts or occurrences, or to watch carefully. In the process of scientific inquiry, observation uses ALL the senses.

Pay attention to events and facts with your senses of sight, smell, touch, taste, and hearing. *(But do NOT taste substances other than foods. Also, make sure you touch and smell things only if you are sure they are safe.)*

1. Get a friend to rest his (or her) arm on a table with an open hand over the edge. Hold a dollar bill (half of it above his hand) between his thumb and fingers. The friend's job is to grab the dollar bill when you let go. Do not let him know when you are going to let it go. Now, let go!

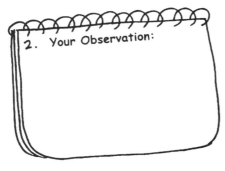

2. Put a drop of lemon juice on your tongue. Immediately drop a bit of baking powder on the same spot on your tongue.

3. Press your first two fingers gently against the right side of your neck just next to your Adam's apple.

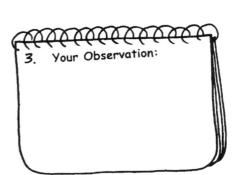

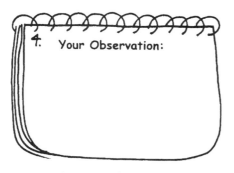

4. Rub your hands together very hard and fast.

Use with page 41.

Name _____

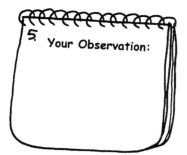

5. Cook a raw egg (in its shell) in boiling water for 10 minutes. Drop it into cool water. As soon as you can handle the egg, peel it. Smash the egg yolk with a fork.

6. Get a glass (made of glass) and a square of cardboard or construction paper larger than the top of the glass. Fill the glass all the way to the top with water. Place the cardboard over the top. Hold you hand over the top of the cardboard as you quickly flip the glass upside down. Then take your hand away from the cardboard.

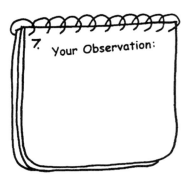

7. Set two ice cubes on separate plates. Lay a white cloth or paper towel over one. Lay a black cloth over the other. Check on them every few minutes.

8. Peel a green banana. Slice a chunk off the banana and eat it.

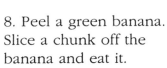

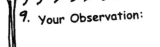

9. Open a bottle of cider vinegar.

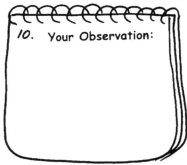

10. Fill a metal cup with ice water. Wrap your hands around the cup and hold it.

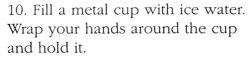

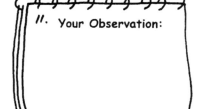

11. Open a brand new bottle of soda pop.

Use with page 40.

Name

41 *Basic Skills/Science Concepts & Processes 4-5*

SCIENCE IS A CLASSY SUBJECT

To **CLASSIFY**

is to assign objects, events, systems, or processes to a group or category based on a common characteristic.

Francine's science class thinks science has a lot of class! She is right—because putting things into classes is a big part of science.

Join her class in this classification activity. All the items in each list belong to one category.

Write a label that could be used to name the class for each group of items.

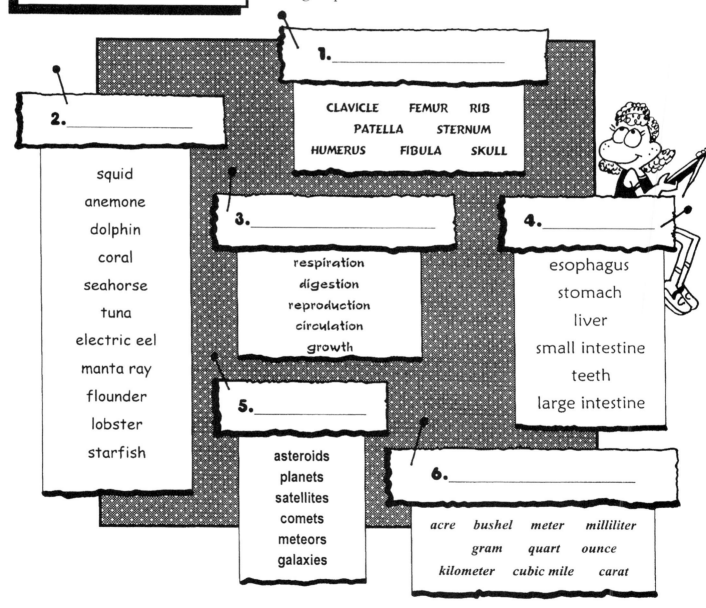

1. _____

CLAVICLE   FEMUR   RIB
PATELLA   STERNUM
HUMERUS   FIBULA   SKULL

2. _____

squid
anemone
dolphin
coral
seahorse
tuna
electric eel
manta ray
flounder
lobster
starfish

3. _____

respiration
digestion
reproduction
circulation
growth

4. _____

esophagus
stomach
liver
small intestine
teeth
large intestine

5. _____

asteroids
planets
satellites
comets
meteors
galaxies

6. _____

acre   bushel   meter   milliliter
gram   quart   ounce
kilometer   cubic mile   carat

Use with page 43.

Name

Answer the questions or follow the directions in each box.

7. Which of these could NOT be classified as minerals? *(Circle them.)*

quartz talc

gold hydrogen

feldspar

garnet topaz neon

graphite sugar

diamond

8.

PINE SPRUCE FIR
CEDAR HEMLOCK JUNIPER

Which of these labels are correct for the items above? *(Circle them.)*

conifers deciduous trees

trees seed-bearing plants

gymnosperms living things

9. Which of these could NOT be classified as insects? *(Circle them.)*

crayfish centipede earthworm

beetle mosquito scorpion

lightning bug grasshopper

spider housefly

inchworm ladybug ant

10. Which of these would be in a group labeled *Herbivores*?

rabbit

owl

lion

shark

caterpillar

deer

raccoon

cow

elephant

hyena

squirrel

human

frog

rattlesnake crocodile lizard alligator
gecko iguana python
boa constrictor

Write two different correct labels that could be used to classify the items above.

11. _____

12. _____

Use with page 42.

Name

SMART GUESSING

To **HYPOTHESIZE**
is to make an assumption
in order to test
an idea further.

Hypothesizing is more than just guessing. A hypothesis is a smart guess that you make after you gather some information through careful observation of facts and events.

Read the description of each event. Then make a smart guess (hypothesis) about it. Make sure the hypothesis is something that could be tested through scientific inquiry.

Example

Zeke filled a water bottle to the top and screwed the top on tightly. He set it in the bottom of his backpack. Later, he dropped the backpack on a sharp rock. The rock punctured the backpack and poked a small hole in the bottom of the bottle. But the water did not come out of the hole!

Hypothesis: *Air will not flow out of a bottle unless there is air inside it to push it out.*

Zeke just loved to eat deli turkey. Sometimes he fed a bit of it to his cat. He noticed that his cat came running every time he opened the plastic deli bag!

1. Your hypothesis: _____

_____

_____

_____

Zeke decided to have some fun playing with two eggs from the refrigerator. He noticed that a cooked egg did a nice, smooth spin. A fresh egg wobbled when he tried to spin it!

2. Your hypothesis: _____

_____

_____

_____

Use with page 45.

Name

At a birthday party, Zeke and his friends were banging on their glasses of punch. They thought it was fun to make a lot of noise. Then they noticed that different glasses made different sounds. They also noticed that different glasses had different amounts of punch in them.

3. Your hypothesis: _____

_____

_____

_____

Zeke tried to make homemade ice cream. He followed the recipe, but forgot to put the salt on the ice that was around the tin of liquid ice cream mixture. He turned the crank on the machine for a long time, but the ice cream never froze.

4. Your hypothesis: _____

_____

_____

_____

Zeke had a small plastic bottle with a straw fitted tightly through the top. He drank all the pop out through the straw. Then he continued sucking on the straw. Pretty soon the plastic bottle collapsed!

5. Your hypothesis: _____

_____

_____

_____

Zeke was fooling around with his silverware at supper. He hit his metal fork with the metal spoon, and the fork made a singing sound. Soon, the sound stopped. He absentmindedly put the fork between his teeth. He started to hear the singing sound again!

6. Your hypothesis: _____

_____

_____

_____

Use with page 44.

Name _____

DON'T FORGET THE MATH!

Max needs to answer each of these science questions.

Tell how he might use math as a part of his process for each one.

To USE NUMBERS

Numbers are used constantly in science. Numbers are needed for measurements. They describe amounts. And they are used in many math operations needed for science.

To MEASURE

is to compare an object to some standard quantity in order to find out an amount or an extent.

1. How quickly do fruit flies multiply in one week? _____

_____

2. One plant sits in the sun and one sits in the dark for two weeks. Both are kept moist. How much more does one plant grow than the other in that time?

_____

3. How long will it take for a rat to find its way through a maze with food at the exit?

_____

4. Max counted 32 ants outside an anthill. He's told that there are probably 100 times as many inside. How many ants are probably in this area all together?

_____

5. Max needs to take 800 sugar cubes to school for his science lesson. Each cube is one square inch. Can he fit the cubes into his backpack?

_____

6. What is the difference between the temperature of his soda pop straight from a warm can and the soda pop that's been poured over ice cubes?

_____

7. How much salt is needed in a cup of water to make an egg float?

_____

Name

INSTEAD OF THE REAL THING

Sometimes you can't examine the real thing! You might not be able to look inside a tooth, or get a close-up view of an erupting volcano. You might not have the tools to look at an atom, or use a spaceship to get a view of the Earth.

When you want to study something that you can't see or hold or examine up close, you can make a model. This will help you learn about how that object or event really works.

> To **USE MODELS** is to use some sort of a structure that visually represents real objects or events.

1. Axel built a model of a volcano. He put 1/2 cup of baking soda in a bottle. Then he formed a clay mountain around the bottle. Finally, he squirted in a bit of liquid dish detergent, and poured 1/2-cup of vinegar into the bottle. What might this help him learn or understand?

_____

_____

_____

2. Dr. Gravity uses graham crackers and frosting to make a model of the plates on which Earth's crust rests. She spreads frosting on a cookie sheet. She can move the crackers around on the frosting. What might this help her learn or understand?

_____

_____

_____

_____

What might this help her students learn or understand?

_____

_____

_____

Name

47   _Basic Skills/Science Concepts & Processes 4-5_

WHAT? WHY? WHAT ELSE?

Felicia has finished an experiment, and she has some results.

To INFER
is to draw a conclusion based on facts or information gained from careful study.

To PREDICT
is to foretell what is likely to happen based on an observation or an experiment.

Now she needs to do something with the results. What do they mean? What has she learned from them? What do the results suggest about other things that might happen? How can she share the results?

Read the results. Help me make inferences, predictions, and interpretations from those results.
(Read the definitions in all the boxes on pages 48 and 49.)

THE QUESTION: How does the amount of water in a bottle affect the sound that can be made by blowing across the top of the bottle?

THE EXPERIMENT: Eight identical 12-inch tall bottles were filled with water to randomly different levels. Felicia made sure no two bottles had the same amount of water. She measured the amount in each bottle and wrote the measurement on the outside of the bottle with a marker. Then Felicia blew across the top of each bottle and listened to the sound. She arranged the bottles in order of the sounds (from lowest to highest pitch). Then she rated the pitches 1-8 in order of pitch from low to high. She kept a chart of measurements and the pitches.

THE RESULTS: The lowest sounds were produced by blowing on the bottle that had the smallest amount of water (½ inch). The highest pitches resulted from blowing on the bottle that was nearly full (8 inches).

1. What can you infer about the connection between the amount of water in the bottles and the pitch of the sound that results from blowing on them? _____

_____

2. How could Felicia show or communicate her results? _____

_____

3. What can you predict about the sound that would result from an identical bottle that has 9 1/2 inches of water in it?

_____

_____

4. How would you interpret these results?

_____

_____

Use with page 49.

Name _____

To **INTERPRET**
is to explain or tell the meaning of the results in an experiment.

To **COMMUNICATE**
is to tell or show others the process and results of the experiment.

Axel has been doing a great balloon trick experiment. He's having fun watching what happened. But he may not learn anything from the experiment if he doesn't try to explain the results. No one else will learn from his experiment if he doesn't communicate the results and their meaning.

Read the results. Help me infer, interpret, and communicate my results.
(Read all the definitions in the boxes on pages 48 and 49.)

OBSERVATION: Axel noticed a swooshing sound every time he opened a bottle of soda pop. He knew that soda contains a gas, carbon dioxide.

THE HYPOTHESIS: Gas confined in a small space will easily escape to another space.

THE EXPERIMENT: Axel planned to make gas in a bottle and try to find out what would happen to the gas in the bottle when the bottle had no top to hold the gas in. He put some vinegar in a bottle. He put some baking soda into a small, stretchy balloon (not inflated). Then he stretched the balloon end over the top of the bottle. Carefully, he lifted the balloon straight up so that the baking soda would pour into the vinegar.

THE RESULTS: After the baking soda dumped into the vinegar, the balloon slowly inflated.

5. What can you infer about the cause of the swooshing sound from the soda pop bottle? _____

_____

6. What do you predict will happen if he repeats the experiment with a larger balloon and a larger amount of baking soda and vinegar? _____

_____

7. How would you interpret (explain) the results of the experiment? _____

_____

_____

8. Describe a way Axel could communicate (share or show) his results. _____

_____

_____

Use with page 48.

Name _____

LOOKING FOR ANSWERS

> ### To **DESIGN AN EXPERIMENT**
> is to make a plan in order to find an answer for a question or to test a hypothesis. The plan includes all the steps to take and the equipment to be used in the experiment.

Dr. Gravity loves chocolate milk and hot chocolate. When she puts some cocoa powder in her cold milk one day, the powder did not dissolve. When she tried the same powder in hot milk, it dissolved completely. She guessed that other substances would dissolve better in hot water than in cold water.

So, Dr. Gravity designed an experiment. She planned to mix several different powders in hot and cold water. She bought flour, sugar, baking powder, cornstarch, cinnamon, pepper, lemonade powder, powdered milk, and baby powder. She gathered supplies: 18 containers of the same size, measuring spoons and a measuring cup, 9 spoons for mixing, and hot and cold water.

She planned to put 1 cup of cold water into 9 cups and 1 cup of hot water into 9 cups. Then she would mix 1 tablespoon of each substance into hot water and cold water.

She also made a chart and planned to write a description of how each substance mixed into the hot and cold water.

1. What was Dr. Gravity's hypothesis? _____

_____

2. What equipment did she plan to use? _____

_____

3. What step in the plan would follow putting water in the containers? _____

_____

4. How did her plan include the use of numbers? _____

_____

Use with page 51.

Name _____

Archie hates bugs. His house seems to be overrun by spiders, ants, and flies. When he visits the homes of his friends, he doesn't see as many bugs. He realizes that all his friends have a cat. He wonders if a cat in the house results in fewer bugs.

Design an experiment or investigation Archie could carry out to help him answer his question.

QUESTION:

_____
_____
_____

HYPOTHESIS:

_____
_____
_____

TOOLS & SUPPLIES:

_____
_____
_____

STEPS FOR INVESTIGATION: _____

_____
_____
_____
_____
_____
_____
_____
_____
_____
_____

HOW RESULTS WILL BE SHOWN: _____

_____
_____
_____

Use with page 50.

Name

CONFUSION IN THE LAB

One of the science students was asked to make a chart of safety rules for the lab. This student had some trouble with the rules. Beware! There is something TERRIBLY WRONG with every one of them. Find her mistakes and fix them. Cross out words or correct the rule in the space above it.

LAB SAFETY RULES

1. Keep a fire blanket, fire extinguisher, and first aid kit in the next room.

2. Wear goggles and an apron unless you are heating, pouring, or using chemicals.

3. Always slant a test tube toward you when you are heating a substance.

4. If you spill anything on your clothes or skin, wash it off after class.

5. It is not important to tie back loose hair when working in the lab.

6. Use whatever equipment you can find, including kitchen utensils.

7. If your clothes catch on fire, run from the lab immediately.

Ouch!

8. Inhale materials and chemicals to see if they are safe.

9. Taste substances by putting a tiny bit on your tongue.

10. Only eat out of lab containers after you wash them.

11. Wear baggy sleeves whenever you work in the lab.

12. Don't bother the teacher by telling about injuries.

13. Clean up by washing all the materials down the sink.

Name

APPENDIX

CONTENTS

Terms for Science Concepts & Processes 54

Some Fields of Science 55

Science Concepts & Processes Skills Test 56

Skills Test Answer Key 60

Answers to Exercises 61

TERMS FOR
SCIENCE CONCEPTS & PROCESSES

cause — anything that brings about a result

change — the process of becoming different

classify — to put objects or processes in a group or category based on common characteristic or group of characteristics

communicate — tell or show others the steps and results of an experiment

constancy — a state characterized by a lack of variation

cycle — a series of events or operations that occurs regularly and usually leads back to the starting point

effect — a result; an event or situation that follows from a cause

experiment — a planned series of steps designed to find an answer to a question

form — the shape or other physical characteristics of an object, organism, or system

form & function — the relationship between the shape (form) of an object, organism, or system and its operation (function)—usually a relationship where the function is dependent upon the form

function — the operation of an object organism, or system

energy-matter — the close relationships and interactions between matter and energy

hypothesize — to make an assumption or a careful guess in order to test it further

infer — to draw a conclusion based on facts or information gained from an inquiry

interpret — to explain or tell the meaning of the results of an investigation

investigation — an experiment or other organized plan for answering a question

measure — to compare an object or amount to a standard quantity in order to find out an amount or an extent

model — a structure that visually represents real objects or events

observe — to recognize facts or occurrences; to watch carefully

order — the predictable behavior of objects, units or matter, events, organisms, or systems

organization — the arrangement of independent items, objects, organisms, units of matter or systems, jointed into a whole system or structure

predict — to foretell what is likely to happen based on an observation or experiment

scientific inquiry — a way of doing investigations and looking for explanations about happenings in the physical world; a series of steps generally followed in looking for answers to questions in science

system — an organized group of related parts that form a whole, working together to perform one or more functions

A SHORT SUMMARY OF THE TOPICS STUDIED BY SOME FIELDS OF SCIENCE

aeronautics — the operation of aircraft

agronomy — soils and crop production

anatomy — the structure of organisms

anthropology — human cultures

archaeology — past current cultures

astronomy — space bodies and their motions

bacteriology — bacteria and their relation to medicine, health, and agriculture

biology — living organisms and life processes

botany — plants

chemistry — properties, structure, and make-up of substances, and the changes they undergo

climatology — climate

cryogenics — behavior of substances at very low temperatures

cytology — the structure and behavior of cells

ecology — the interrelationship of organisms and their environment

embryology — embryos and their development

entomology — insects

genetics — heredity and variations in organisms

geography — earth features and their relationship to the living things on earth

geology — history of the earth

hematology — blood and blood-forming organs

histology — living tissues

hydrology — water in the atmosphere and on the land surface, in soil, and in rocks

ichthyology — fish

immunology — causes of immunity

linguistics — human speech

marine biology — ocean life

meteorology — weather

microbiology — living organisms too small to be seen with the naked eye

neurology — nervous system

oceanology — ocean characteristics, processes, behaviors, and life

oncology — tumors

pathology — diseases

paleontology — fossils and the life from past geological periods

petrology — origin, structure, properties, classification, and history of rocks

physics — matter and energy and their interactions

physiology — the function of living organisms

radiology — use of radiant energy to diagnose and treat diseases

rheumatology — diseases characterized by inflammation and pain in joints or muscles

seismology — earthquakes

sociology — behavior of human groups and of humans in groups

taxonomy — scientific classification of plants and animals

Name _____

SCIENCE CONCEPTS & PROCESSES
SKILLS TEST

Each correct answer is worth 1 point. Total possible points: 46

1–12: Which field of science matches each topic below? Write a letter from the list.

_____ 1. earth history

_____ 2. blood

_____ 3. elements & compounds

_____ 4. cells

_____ 5. fish

_____ 6. diseases

_____ 7. body processes

_____ 8. human cultures

_____ 9. plants

_____ 10. birds

_____ 11. earthquakes

_____ 12. weather

A. pathology
B. cytology
C. ecology
D. hematology
E. paleontology
F. ichthyology
G. anthropology
H. geology
I. physiology
J. zoology
K. ornithology
L. chemistry
M. botany
N. seismology
O. meteorology

13–18: Decide which statements below are true. Circle their numbers.

13. Science is the study of the ways in which the universe works.

14. Scientific discoveries began thousands of years ago.

15. The field of seismology would fall into the life science branch.

16. Paper was invented before the telescope.

17. Genetics, zoology, and botany are all life sciences.

18. Science can solve any human problem.

Name _____

19–21: Write a rule for science safety related to each of the following:

19. holding a test tube while
    heating a substance in it _____

20. tasting substances in science lab _____

21. if your clothes catch fire during a science experiment _____

22–26: Circle one correct answer:

22. The 1898, John P. Holland invented the _____, giving humans a new way to travel through water.

a. sailboat   b. jet ski   c. submarine   d. ocean liner   e. SCUBA tank

23. The microwave oven was invented

a. before 1900.   b. in the mid-1900s.   c. after 2000.   d. before 1800.

24. Which was discovered first?

a. fire   b. gravity   c. the atom   d. the shape of planet Earth   e. human DNA

25. Who discovered an element that led to the production of atomic energy?

a. Thomas Edison   b. Louis Pasteur   c. Galileo   d. Marie and Pierre Curie

26. The first step in scientific inquiry is

a. gathering data.   b. making an observation.   c. making predictions.   d. starting a hypothesis.

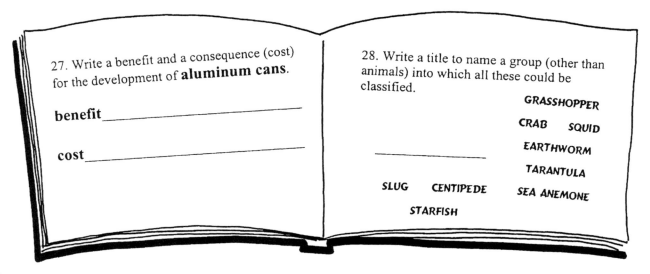

27. Write a benefit and a consequence (cost) for the development of **aluminum cans**.

benefit_____

cost_____

28. Write a title to name a group (other than animals) into which all these could be classified.

_____

GRASSHOPPER

CRAB   SQUID

EARTHWORM

TARANTULA

SLUG   CENTIPEDE   SEA ANEMONE

STARFISH

Name

29–35. Which Big Idea (science concept) is shown by each of these examples? Write the code letter or letters of one big idea on the line in front of each number. (There may be more than one right answer for each.)

_____ 29. A stick of butter left in the sun will soon become liquid.

_____ 30. Car # 1 hits car # 2. This pushes car # 2 into car # 3, which is forced off the road.

_____ 31. Living things are divided into two major groups called kingdoms.

_____ 32. Every electron (a kind of particle in an atom) has a negative electric charge.

_____ 33. When baking soda is mixed with vinegar, carbon dioxide is produced.

_____ 34. The heart pumps blood around the body through a network of arteries, veins, and capillaries.

_____ 35. Dandelion seeds have fluffy tops so light that they can float on the wind.

BIG IDEAS
(Science Concepts)

ORG	Organization
F	Form & Function
C-E	Cause & Effect
E-M	Energy-Matter
C	Constancy
CY	Cycle
CH	Change
S	Systems
ORD	Order

36–39. Give an example of each of the following:

36. a cycle in life science _____

37. a cause-effect relationship in Earth science _____

_____

38. an interaction between matter and energy _____

_____

39. an item whose form affects its function

_____

Great Inventors

Name

OBSERVATION: At the picnic, there are more flies on the meat platter than on any of the salads.

40. Read the observation.
    Write a hypothesis that could be tested.

_____

_____

_____

Francie noticed how easily she could float in the ocean. This was much easier than floating in a lake or swimming pool. She guessed that things must float more easily in salt water than in fresh water.

She decided to do an experiment. She found two small jars. She measured exactly two cups of warm water into each jar. Then she placed one egg in each jar. Both eggs sank to the bottom of the jar.

She stirred one tablespoon of salt into each jar. She continued to stir one tablespoon at a time into the first jar. After she added 3 tablespoons, the egg began to float. She stirred 6 tablespoons into the second jar. The egg in the second jar floated higher in the water than the first egg.

Francie concluded that things do float better in salt water. She also concluded that objects floated higher in the water as the salt content increased. She thought the reason for this was that salt water has greater density than fresh water. (The molecules are closer together.)

41—46. Read about Francie's experiment. Write your answer to each question.

41. What observation led to the experiment? _____

42. What was her hypothesis? _____

43. What were the results?_____

44. How did she explain the results? _____

45. What results would you predict if she repeated the experiment with lemons? _____

_____

46. How could Francie share or communicate her results? _____

Name

SKILLS TEST ANSWER KEY

1. E or H

2. D

3. L

4. B

5. F

6. A or C or H

7. I

8. G

9. M

10. K

11. N

12. O

13–18: The true statements are 13, 14, 16, and 17.

19–21: Answers will vary somewhat.

19. Always point a test tube away from yourself when heating a substance.

20. Do not taste any substances unless the teacher tells you to.

21. Roll on the floor or roll in a blanket. Do not run.

22. c

23. b

24. a

25. d

26. b

27. Answers will vary: Check to see that student has written an appropriate benefit and cost.

28. Answers will vary: All are animals without back-bones. All have legs or tentacles.

29–35: Answers may vary. Give credit for any choice student can explain.

29. CH or E-M

30. E-M or C-E

31. ORG or ORD

32. C or E-M

33. CH or C-E

34. S or E-M

35. F-F

36–39. Answers will vary. Give students credit for sensible, accurate answers.

40. Answers will vary. Hypothesis may be something such as: Meat attracts more flies than non-meat foods.

41. She floated easily in salt water.

42. Things float better in salt water than in fresh water.

43. The egg did not float in fresh water, but did float in salt water. The saltier the water, the higher the egg floated.

44. Salt water is more dense than fresh water.

45. The lemons would probably float in salt water if enough salt were added.

46. Answers will vary. Give credit for a sensible suggestion for communicating results.

ANSWERS TO EXERCISES

Answers to Exercises

pages 10–11

1–14. Answers will vary. Check to see that student has given descriptions that clearly include a science example.

page 12

Lawrence has the following correct (These should be circled):
1, 2, 3, 5, 7, 9, 10
Lester has the following correct:
4, 6, 8

page 13

Answers may vary. These fields may have connections with more than one branch. Allow any answers which are sensible, and which student can explain.

1. L	9. E-S
2. P, or E-S	10. L
3. L	11. P
4. L or E-S	12. P
5. L	13. E-S
6. L	14. P
7. E-S	15. L
8. E-S or L	

pages 14–15

1. a	12. a
2. c	13. c
3. c	14. c
4. b	15. a
5. a	16. b
6. b	17. c
7. a	18. b
8. a	19. b
9. c	20. c
10. b	21. b
11. b	

pages 16–17

1. maps	10. fax machine
2. microscope	11. electricity
3. wheel	12. anesthetics
4. telescope	13. sewing machine
5. printing press	14. telegraph
6. penicillin	15. gravity
7. parachute	16. submarine
8. refrigerator	17. paper
9. frozen food process	18. x-rays

pages 18–19

1–14: Answers will vary. Check to see that student has given a reasonable explanation for each one.

pages 20–21

1. b	7. b
2. b	8. c
3. d	9. d
4. b	10. a and b
5. a	11. a, c, and d
6. a	12. c

pages 22–23

1–12 Answers will vary. Check to see that student has written a reasonable benefit and cost for each example.

pages 24–25

Answers will vary somewhat.
1. The bananas ripened at different rates.
2. What causes some bananas to ripen faster than others?
3. Bananas ripen more quickly when uncovered or touching other bananas.
4. Testing bananas in different groups to watch ripening time: out of bags, with other fruit, and in paper or plastic bags.
5. green bananas, ripe bananas, paper bags, plastic bags, tape
6. Uncovered bananas ripened most quickly. Bananas touching other bananas ripen quickest.

Bananas ripen faster in paper bags than in plastic bags.
7. Air causes bananas to ripen faster; bananas give off a substance that makes other bananas (touching) ripen faster.
8. He used a poster to show the experiment and results.
9. Did opening the paper bags affect ripening time? How fast would green bananas ripen out in a basket with no ripe fruit touching them? How fast would a banana ripen in the refrigerator?

pages 26–27

Answers may vary somewhat. Accept any answer that is reasonable or that student can explain.
Change: 1, 2, 3, 4, 11, 12, 13
Constancy: 2, 7, 16
System: 3, 5, 7, 9
Order: 2, 4, 7, 13, 15
Organization: 14
Cause-Effect: 1, 6, 8, 9, 11, 12
Form-Function: 5, 10
Energy-Matter: 1, 6, 8, 10, 11
Cycle: 1, 2, 7, 13, 15

page 28

Answers may vary somewhat. Students do not have to list all the parts of a system. Accept answers that are reasonable.
1. Parts: lungs, trachea, bronchial tubes, bronchi, alveoli, diaphragm, blood vessels
Input: air or oxygen
Output: carbon dioxide
2. Parts: leaves, stems, roots
Input: sunshine, air, water, carbon dioxide
Output: oxygen
3. Parts: light bulb, battery, wires
Input: electricity
Output: light

page 29

Answers may vary on 1 and 2. Accept reasonable answers.
1. They'll get closer together.
2. storing up food
3. 5, 2, 3, 1, 6, 4
4. vertebrates, invertebrates
5. angiosperms, gymnosperms

6.

8 (Neptune)	3 (Earth)
4 (Mars)	2 (Venus)
9 (Pluto)	7 (Uranus)
1 (Mercury)	6 (Saturn)
5 (Jupiter)	

pages 30–31

Answers may vary somewhat. There are many possible categories for A–J. Allow any reasonable answers for 1–6.
1. B, F, I, or J
2. D or E
3. B, D, or I
4. A, C, G, or J
5. A, H, or I
6. G

7–12: Answers will vary. Accept any answer that is an accurate example of the requirement.

pages 32–33

Answers may vary somewhat. Accept answers that are clearly causes and effects. There may be more than one possibility of a cause-effect pair for some examples.
1. *cause:* Magma gushes out.
   effect: A volcano is formed.
2. *cause:* Lava cooled quickly.
   effect: Air was trapped inside and pumice is light.
   OR
   cause: Air was trapped inside.
   effect: Pumice is light.
3. *cause:* He ran for 6 months.
   effect: His heart rate fell.
4. *cause:* A singer used her voice a lot.
   effect: Bumps formed on her vocal cords.
   OR
   cause: A singer used her voice a lot.
   effect: Her voice became hoarse and scratchy.
   OR
   cause: Bumps formed on her vocal cords.
   effect: voice became hoarse and scratchy.
5. *cause:* The rattlesnake senses the presence of predator.
   effect: The rattlesnake rattles its tail.
   OR
   cause: The rattlesnake senses a

predator and rattles its tail.
   effect: The predator runs away.
   OR
   cause: The predator hears the warning.
   effect: The predator runs away.

6–10: Answers will vary. Accept answers that are reasonable possibilities.
6. *effect:* The rock breaks apart.
7. *effect:* coughing or choking
8. *cause:* Axel takes an antibiotic.
9. *cause:* The meteoroid enters Earth's atmosphere.
10. Answers will vary.

pages 34–35

Answers may vary somewhat.
1. *function:* can catch and trap insects
2. *function:* allows bird to be light enough to stay in air
3. *function:* can close to keep food out of trachea
4. *function:* can wedge into wood
5. *function:* is able to creep along surfaces
6. *function:* protects the softer insides of teeth
7. *function:* can expand to hold food
8. *form:* have stiff cell walls
9. *form:* muscular, can relax and contract
10. *form:* They stick to surfaces; allow fly to crawl up things.
11. *form:* shaped like a funnel
    function: catches sounds
12. Check to see that student has given reasonable example of an object and the connection between form and function.

pages 36–37

Answers may vary somewhat. Accept any reasonable answers.
1. *matter:* skin
   energy: sun's heat
   result: Skin will burn.
2. *matter:* branch
   energy: gravity
   result: Branch will fall to ground.
3. *matter:* popcorn kernels
   energy: heat
   result: Kernels will explode.
4. *matter:* people, rope
   energy: people's muscle power
   result: Lighter team will be

dragged across line.
5. *matter:* raft
   energy: power of moving water
   result: The raft will be tossed around.
6. *matter:* cabin
   energy: power of moving air
   result: The cabin will be damaged.
7. *matter:* space ship
   energy: gravity
   result: Satellite will stay in orbit.
8. *matter:* hat
   energy: moving air
   result: Hat will blow away.
9. Answers will vary.

pages 38–39

Explanations of the cycle will vary somewhat. Give students credit for answers that show general, simple understanding of the cycle.

1. *Butterfly Life Cycle:* The adult butterfly lays eggs. The eggs grow into a wormlike larva (or caterpillar). The caterpillar eats and grows. Then it forms a covering abound itself (a pupa). Inside the pupa an adult butterfly forms and hatches. Again, this adult lays eggs.
2. *Oxygen-Carbon Dioxide Cycle:* Plants take carbon dioxide from the air and make oxygen through photosynthesis. The plants give off the oxygen. Humans and other animals take in the oxygen and breathe out carbon dioxide, which the plants use.
3. *Frog Life Cycle:* A female adult frog lays eggs that are fertilized by the male. These eggs grow into tadpoles, which gradually lose their tails and change into adult frogs. The adults lay eggs and the cycle begins again.
4. *Moon Phases:* The appearance of the moon (from earth) changes depending on the moon's position in relation to the Earth and sun. A new moon (where the dark side of the moon is facing Earth) occurs when the moon is between the sun and Earth. As the moon moves in its orbit, more of the sunlit side

becomes visible until it is fully visible. As it continues to move, less of the sunlit side becomes visible, until it is back in the new moon position.

5. *Earth's Revolution:* The earth travels in a path called an orbit (elliptical in shape) around the sun. It takes about 365 days for the earth to travel and arrive back at its starting point. *Other cycles:* Answers will vary.

pages 40–41

Answers may vary somewhat. Accept any reasonable answers that show observations from any of the senses.

1. The money falls; the friend cannot grab it.
2. The baking powder takes away the bitter lemon taste.
3. There is a regular thumping under the skin.
4. The hands get warm.
5. There is a strong smell.
6. The cardboard stays; the water does not spill out.
7. The ice cube under the black cloth melts faster than the other.
8. The banana tastes bitter.
9. The cup feels very cold.
10. There is a sharp, acid smell.
11. I hear a fizzy or "whooshing" sound.

pages 42–43

1–6 Answers may vary. Accept any label that accurately describes a class containing ALL items.

1. bones in the human body
2. sea animals, animals
3. human body processes; animal processes
4. body parts, body organs, or organs in the digestive system
5. space features or objects
6. units of measurement
7. hydrogen, neon, sugar
8. conifers, trees, gymnosperms, seed-bearing plants, living things
9. crayfish, centipede, earthworm, scorpion, spider, inchworm
10. rabbit, caterpillar, deer, cow, elephant, squirrel

11–12: Answers may vary. Accept any label that accurately describes classes containing ALL items. Some possibilities

are: reptiles, vertebrates, animals with scales, cold-blooded animals

pages 44–45

Answers will vary. Possibilities are suggested. Accept any hypothesis that is reasonable given the observation.

1. Cats will respond to sounds that are connected with food.
2. Cooked eggs will spin with a regular spin. Fresh eggs will not.
3. The amount of water in a glass container determines the pitch of a sound made when the glass is struck with a spoon.
4. Salt lowers the temperature of ice.
5. A container will collapse when the air inside it is removed.
6. Sound travels through teeth.

page 46

Answers may vary. Accept any reasonable answers.

1. counting flies at beginning and end of one week
2. measuring change in plant size
3. measuring time
4. counting ants, multiplying
5. calculating the volume of the backpack
6. measuring temperature
7. measuring water and salt

page 47

Answers may vary. Accept any answer that shows student understands the value of the model.

1. how melted rock (lava) flows out of a volcano when the volcano erupts
2. how plates on Earth's crust move, overlap, slide against each other, or break

pages 48–49

Answers may vary. Accept any reasonable answers.

1. The pitch becomes higher as the amount of water increases.
2. Answers will vary.
3. The sound will have a higher pitch than any other.

4. Answers will vary. (Possibility: Different amounts of air left above the water have different rates of vibration, causing different sounds.)
5. Gas is escaping from the bottle.
6. The balloon will inflate.
7. Answers will vary. (Possibility: The molecules from gas can spread apart easily to fill a different space.)
8. Answers will vary.

pages 50–51

1. Substances dissolve more easily in hot water than in cold water.
2. 18 containers, measuring cup and spoons, spoons for mixing, hot and cold water, substances to mix: flour, sugar, baking powder, cornstarch, cinnamon, pepper, lemonade mix, powdered mile, baby powder
3. mixing 1 tablespoon of each substance into hot and cold water
4. counting containers, measuring water and substances

page 52

The changes made may vary somewhat; but they should contain these general ideas:

1. Keep these three things in the SAME room (not next room).
2. Wear goggles and apron WHEN (not unless) you work with chemicals.
3. Slant the test tube AWAY from yourself (not toward).
4. Wash off spills RIGHT AWAY (not after class).
5. Cross out the word NOT.
6. USE ONLY LAB EQUIPMENT (not use any equipment).
7. LIE DOWN and ROLL or roll up in a blanket (not run).
8. Add NEVER to the beginning of the sentence.
9. NEVER taste substances unless directed by a teacher.
10. DON'T eat out of lab containers (not ONLY).
11. Add DON'T to the beginning of the sentence.
12. Tell the teacher about ALL injuries.
13. DON'T wash materials down the sink.